Sanjeev Kapoor

HIGH FIBRE RECIPES

The key to leading a healthy life

In association with Alyona Kapoor

Popular Prakashan
www.popularprakashan.com

Published by
POPULAR PRAKASHAN PVT. LTD.
301, Mahalaxmi Chambers
22, Bhulabhai Desai Road
Mumbai - 400 026

First Published 2017

(4478)
ISBN: 978-81-7991-919-4

Design: Anjali Sawant

PRINTED IN INDIA
by Saurabh Printers (P) Ltd.
Plot No. 67 A-68, Ecotech, Ext. I
Kasna, Greater Noida-201306 (U.P)

Author's Note

A high fibre diet keeps our digestive system clean and healthy and also flushes cholesterol and harmful carcinogens out of our body. It not only aids our digestive system but also lowers the risk of heart disease, stroke and diabetes – the three most common lifestyle diseases that can mar the quality of our lives. High fibre diet is also known to improve the health of our skin and help us lose weight.

But what is fibre? In simple words it is roughage that is a part of plant-based foods like grains, fruits, vegetables, nuts and beans.

In *High Fibre Recipes - The key to leading a healthy life* I have compiled delicious recipes that have good quantity of fibre. Sprouts and Apple Salad, Sweetcorn Chicken Soup, Baked Corn Rolls, Kadai Vegetables, Palak Raita, Bikaneri Dal Parantha and Gajar aur Khajur Halwa are a few recipes from this collection.

Each recipe serves four portions when it is a part of a menu comprising of other dishes. Whatever you cook and eat, always remember the key word is 'moderation'. Everything in moderation is good for health and anything in excess has the opposite effect.

Happy cooking!

Contents

Amrud Ka Sherbet

INGREDIENTS

2 large guavas, chopped

¼ cup sugar

2 inches ginger, grated

1 tablespoon Chaat Masala (page 94)

METHOD

- Place the guavas in a heavy-bottomed non-stick pan along with the sugar and one and a half cups of water.
- Bring it to a boil and simmer till the guavas are tender. Cool completely and transfer into a mixer jar.
- Add the ginger and blend into a purée. Add the chaat masala and stir.
- Half fill each individual glass with the pulp and top up with chilled water and serve immediately.

Watermelon and Apple Cooler

INGREDIENTS

½ medium watermelon, seeded and cut into cubes

1 medium apple

2 teaspoons powdered sugar

Rock salt to taste

1 teaspoon roasted cumin seeds, coarsely crushed

1 tablespoon fresh mint leaves, chopped + a few sprigs for garnishing

Crushed ice, as required

METHOD

- Combine the watermelon, powdered sugar and rock salt in a blender and blend till smooth.
- Transfer into a jar, add crushed cumin seeds, chopped mint and ice and stir to mix well.
- Peel and grate the apple. Add the grated apple to the watermelon, stir, pour into individual glasses and serve garnished with mint sprigs.

INGREDIENTS

2 cups corn kernels

2 tablespoons butter

2 medium green capsicums, roasted, peeled and chopped

4 cups Vegetable Stock (page 95)

Salt to taste

2 teaspoons lemon juice

2 teaspoons chopped fresh coriander

Bhuni Makai ka Soup

METHOD

- Dry-roast the corn kernels in a non-stick pan for five to six minutes.
- Heat the butter in a deep non-stick pan. Add the capsicums and sauté for two minutes.
- Add the roasted corn kernels and sauté for three to four minutes.
- Add the vegetable stock and salt and bring to a boil. Simmer for three to four minutes.
- Take the pan off the heat and allow the contents to cool. Blend coarsely with a hand blender. Add the lemon juice, stir and bring the soup to a boil.
- Serve hot garnished with the chopped coriander.

Bhuni Makai ka Soup

Cream of Asparagus and Almond Soup

Cream of Asparagus and Almond Soup

INGREDIENTS

300 grams asparagus spears

10-12 almonds

Salt to taste

2 tablespoons butter

1 medium onion, chopped

2 tablespoons refined flour

2½ cups Vegetable Stock (page 95)

4-5 black peppercorns, crushed

2 cups milk

METHOD

- Trim the asparagus, discarding the woody part of the stem.
- Cut the remainder into short lengths, reserving a few tips for garnishing.
- Blanch the reserved tips in boiling salted water for one or two minutes. Drain and refresh in cold water.
- Blanch the remaining asparagus in boiling water for two to three minutes. Drain and refresh in cold water. Purée in a blender.
- Broil or dry-roast the almonds over medium heat till the skins change colour slightly. Remove from heat, cool and slice into slivers.

- Melt the butter in a non-stick pan and add the onion. Sauté over a low heat until soft. Stir in the flour and cook for one minute, then gradually add the stock and whisk so that no lumps are formed. Bring the mixture to a boil.
- Simmer for two to three minutes until thickened; stir in the asparagus purée, salt and crushed peppercorns.
- Add the milk and simmer for two to three minutes, stirring continuously.
- Serve hot, garnished with the blanched asparagus tips and almond slivers.

Dal aur Gajar Shorba

INGREDIENTS

½ cup split pigeon peas

2 tablespoons split green gram with skin

2 medium carrots

2-3 whole dried red chillies

6-8 black peppercorns

1 teaspoon cumin seeds

1 teaspoon coriander seeds

4-5 garlic cloves

2 green chillies, slit

Salt to taste

2 tablespoons fresh coriander, chopped

METHOD

- Soak the split pigeon peas in two cups of water and the split green gram with the skin in half a cup of water, separately, for half an hour. Drain.
- Cut one carrot roughly and grate the other coarsely. Set aside. Dry-roast the red chillies, peppercorns, cumin seeds and coriander seeds, and grind together to a coarse powder. Set aside.
- Place the pigeon peas and the green gram in a pressure cooker. Add the roughly cut carrot, garlic and three cups of water, and cook till the lentils are very soft.
- Mash the lentils with a hand blender till smooth. Add one cup of water and green chillies, and bring to a boil. Add the ground spices and salt. Simmer for two minutes.
- Serve, garnished with chopped coriander and grated carrot.

Sweetcorn Chicken Soup

INGREDIENTS

½ cup sweetcorn kernels

150 grams cream-style sweetcorn

1 cup boneless chicken, boiled and shredded

2 tablespoons oil

1 tablespoon chopped cabbage

¼ medium carrot, cut into ½-inch cubes

4-5 cups Chicken Stock (page 94)

3 tablespoons cornflour

Salt to taste

¼ teaspoon white pepper powder

½ tablespoon sugar

¼ teaspoon MSG (optional)

1 stalk spring onion greens, chopped

METHOD

- Heat oil in a non-stick wok or pan. Add cabbage, carrot and corn kernels and stir-fry for a couple of minutes. Add chicken and stir-fry for a couple of minutes more.
- Stir in chicken stock and bring to a boil. Mix in the cream-style sweetcorn and continue cooking for two to three minutes.
- Stir in the salt, white pepper powder, sugar, MSG and the cornflour mixed with half cup of water. Cook on high heat, stirring continuously for one minute or until the soup thickens.
- Serve piping hot, garnished with spring onion greens.

Broccoli and Toasted Almond Soup

INGREDIENTS

400 grams broccoli, separated into small florets

10-12 almonds, roasted and slivered

Salt to taste

4 cups Vegetable Stock (page 95), or water

1 medium onion, roughly chopped

4 garlic cloves, roughly chopped

2 inches celery stalk, chopped

1 cup milk

White pepper powder to taste

METHOD

- Soak the broccoli in salted water for ten to fifteen minutes; drain.
- In a deep non-stick pan, bring the vegetable stock, onion, garlic and celery to a boil.
- Add the broccoli florets and continue to cook, uncovered, for five to seven minutes, or till the broccoli is tender.
- Remove from heat, cool and purée the vegetables in a blender.
- Pour the purée back into the pan and stir in the milk; place on heat and bring the mixture to a boil.
- Season with salt and white pepper powder. Stir in the toasted almond slivers and serve hot.

Baby corn and Avocado Salad

INGREDIENTS

10 baby corn cobs

1 large avocado

2 medium green capsicums, cut into strips

2 large tomatoes, seeded and cut into strips

2 medium cucumbers, cut into strips

DRESSING

4 tablespoons honey

1½ tablespoons lemon juice

5-6 fresh mint leaves, roughly torn

5-6 black peppercorns, crushed

Salt to taste

METHOD

- Cut the baby corn into strips and blanch in boiling water. Drain.
- Gently peel and slice the avocado. Set aside a few slices for garnishing.
- Mix the ingredients for the dressing in a large bowl. Add all the salad ingredients and toss well.
- Place in a refrigerator for twenty to thirty minutes to chill.
- Serve chilled, decorated with avocado slices.

Black Gram and Rice Salad

INGREDIENTS

½ cup black Bengal gram, boiled

1 cup cooked rice

½ cup corn kernels, boiled

¼ medium red capsicum, chopped

1 small onion, chopped

1-2 garlic cloves, crushed

Salt to taste

Black pepper powder to taste

1 tablespoon lemon juice

1 tablespoon olive oil

METHOD

- Place the cooked rice in a bowl.
- Add the Bengal gram, corn, red capsicum, onion, garlic, salt, pepper powder, lemon juice and olive oil, and mix well.
- Serve at once.

Chef's Tip: This salad makes a delicious tiffin-box snack.

Barley and Crunchy Nut Salad

INGREDIENTS

1 cup barley

½ cup peanuts, roasted

2 large cucumbers, seeded, cut into small pieces

2 large tomatoes, seeded, cut into small pieces

2 inches celery stalk, chopped

2 tablespoons chopped fresh coriander

Salt to taste

5-6 black peppercorns, crushed

2 teaspoons lemon juice

4 large lettuce leaves

METHOD

- Soak the barley in three cups of water for six hours.
- Drain and pressure-cook with three cups of water and salt till almost done. Drain and set aside to cool.
- In a large bowl, combine the barley, cucumbers, tomatoes, peanuts, celery, chopped coriander, salt, crushed peppercorns and lemon juice and toss well.
- Arrange the lettuce leaves on a serving platter, transfer the tossed salad onto the lettuce bed and serve immediately.

Barley and Crunchy Nut Salad

Gajar, Kishmish and Black Olive Salad

Gajar, Kishmish and Black Olive Salad

INGREDIENTS

4-5 large carrots

½ cup raisins

6-8 black olives, sliced

2 tablespoons lemon juice

5-6 black peppercorns, crushed

1 green chilli, finely chopped

1 tablespoon honey

Salt to taste

¼ teaspoon black salt

6 walnut kernels, crushed

1 teaspoon extra-virgin olive oil

6-8 fresh mint leaves

METHOD

- Thickly grate carrots. Refrigerate till required for use.
- Combine lemon juice, crushed black peppercorns, green chilli, honey, salt, black salt, walnuts, raisins, black olives and extra-virgin olive oil to make a dressing.
- Just before serving add the dressing to the grated carrots and toss.
- Serve garnished with mint leaves.

INGREDIENTS

1½ cups sweetcorn kernels, boiled and drained

1½ cups boiled red kidney beans

2 spring onions

Salt to taste

Black pepper powder to taste

DRESSING

2 tablespoons Mayonnaise (page 95)

¾ tablespoon mustard paste

2 tablespoons tomato ketchup

½ teaspoon paprika

Corn and Bean Twosome

METHOD

- Chop the spring onion bulbs and greens separately.
- Mix all the ingredients for the dressing with a small wire whisk. Place in a refrigerator to chill.
- Toss the corn, kidney beans and spring onion bulbs in a large bowl.
- Pour the dressing over and season with salt and pepper to taste.
- Sprinkle with the spring onion greens.
- Serve immediately.

Tuna Salad

INGREDIENTS

1 cup drained and flaked tuna

3 pickled onions, chopped

2 inches celery stalk, chopped

4 tablespoons Mayonnaise (page 95)

3 tablespoons tomato ketchup

2 teaspoons red chilli sauce

1 small yellow capsicum, cut into 1-inch cubes

1 small red capsicum, cut into 1-inch cubes

White pepper powder to taste

8 lettuce leaves, hand torn

Salt to taste

METHOD

- Place the tuna in a bowl. Add the pickled onions, celery, mayonnaise, tomato ketchup, red chilli sauce, yellow and red capsicums, white pepper powder and mix.
- Chill the salad in the refrigerator for thirty minutes.
- Arrange the torn lettuce leaves in a bowl. Add salt to the salad and toss. Put the salad over the lettuce leaves and serve.

Sprouts and Apple Salad

INGREDIENTS

1½ cups bean sprouts, blanched

2 apples

6-8 iceberg lettuce

1 medium onion, sliced

1 medium tomato, chopped

DRESSING

2 tablespoons olive oil

¼ cup apple juice

1 tablespoon lemon juice

½ teaspoon black pepper powder

½ teaspoon mustard paste

Salt to taste

METHOD

- Wash and soak the lettuce leaves in ice-cold water for about fifteen minutes.
- To make the dressing, put the olive oil, apple juice, lemon juice, pepper powder, mustard paste and salt in a small bowl and whisk well. Set aside.
- Chop the apples into small pieces. Place them with the sprouts, onion, and tomato in a large bowl.
- Drain the lettuce, tear them into bite-sized pieces, and add them to the sprout mixture and toss.
- Pour the dressing on the salad and toss lightly. Serve immediately.

Chickpea and Red Capsicum Salad

INGREDIENTS

3 cups boiled chickpeas, drained

2 medium red capsicums, roasted

12 black olives, stoned

1 tablespoon chopped fresh parsley

DRESSING

2 tablespoons oil

1 teaspoon grated orange rind

2 tablespoons orange juice

2-3 garlic cloves, crushed

Salt to taste

4-6 black peppercorns, crushed

METHOD

- Keep the chickpeas warm.
- Peel the capsicums. Halve them, remove the core and seeds and slice them thinly.
- Mix all the ingredients for the dressing together.
- Toss the chickpeas while they are still warm into the dressing. Set aside to cool.
- Stir in the capsicums, olives and half the parsley. Transfer the salad to a serving platter and garnish with the remaining parsley.

Chef's Tip: To remove the skins of the capsicums easily, place the hot roasted capsicums in a plastic bag for a few minutes – the steam will loosen the skins.

Green Chana Chaat

INGREDIENTS

1½ cups dried green Bengal gram, soaked overnight

2 medium onions, chopped

2 medium tomatoes, chopped

2-3 green chillies, chopped

2 tablespoons chopped fresh coriander

Black salt to taste

1 teaspoon roasted cumin powder

1 teaspoon Chaat Masala (page 94)

½ teaspoon red chilli powder

2 tablespoons lemon juice

METHOD

- Pressure-cook the soaked gram in three cups of water till the pressure is released two or three times (two or three whistles), or till tender.
- Transfer the green gram to a non-stick kadai and simmer till all the water evaporates.
- Place the hot green gram in a bowl. Add the onions, tomatoes, green chillies, chopped coriander, black salt, roasted cumin powder, chaat masala, chilli powder and lemon juice and mix well. Serve immediately.

Baked Corn Rolls

INGREDIENTS

12 slices of bread with the crusts removed

1 cup boiled sweetcorn

1 large potato, boiled and mashed

2 green chillies, chopped

1 teaspoon ginger paste

¼ cup chopped fresh coriander

1 teaspoon lemon juice

Salt to taste

2 tablespoons oil

1 large onion, chopped

TO SERVE

Green Chutney (page 95)

METHOD

- Preheat the oven to 180°C/350°F/Gas Mark 4.
- Coarsely crush the boiled sweetcorn in a blender. Transfer into a bowl.
- Add the potato, green chillies, ginger paste, chopped coriander, lemon juice and salt and mix well.
- Heat the oil in a non-stick pan and sauté the onion till light brown.

- Add to the corn mixture and mix well. Divide the mixture into twelve equal portions and shape each one into an oval and set aside.
- Soak the slices of bread, one at a time, in water for about ten seconds.
- Squeeze out the excess water by gently pressing each slice between your palms. Place a potato-corn oval at one end of each slice and roll firmly to enclose the oval completely.
- Place the rolls on a greased baking tray.
- Bake for approximately twelve minutes or till the rolls turn light brown.
- Serve hot with tomato ketchup or green chutney.

Baked Corn Rolls

Healthy Cornflake Bhel

Healthy Cornflake Bhel

INGREDIENTS

2 cups cornflakes

1 large potato, boiled, peeled and diced

1 medium onion, chopped

1 large cucumber, seeded and diced

1 large tomato, seeded and diced

1 cup pomegranate kernels

Salt to taste

1 teaspoon Chaat Masala (page 94)

2 tablespoons unripe green mango, chopped

2 tablespoons chopped fresh coriander

2 teaspoons lemon juice

METHOD

- In a large bowl, combine the potato, onion, cucumber, tomato, pomegranate, salt, chaat masala and green mango and toss well to mix.
- Add the cornflakes, chopped coriander and lemon juice and toss again to mix well.
- Transfer the bhel to a serving bowl.
- Serve immediately.

Broken Wheat Upma

INGREDIENTS

1 cup fine broken wheat

¼ cup skimmed milk yogurt

Salt to taste

¼ teaspoon mustard seeds

1 teaspoon skinless split black gram

10-12 curry leaves

1 medium onion, chopped

1 inch ginger, chopped

3-4 green chillies, chopped

1 medium carrot, diced and blanched

¼ cup shelled green peas, blanched

1 teaspoon lemon juice

2 tablespoons chopped fresh coriander

METHOD

- Place the yogurt, salt and three and a half cups of water in a bowl and whisk until smooth. Set aside.
- Heat a non-stick pan; add the mustard seeds and split black gram. When the mustard seeds splutter, add the curry leaves and onion, and cook until lightly browned.
- Stir in the broken wheat and continue to cook on medium heat for two minutes.

- Add the ginger and green chillies, and cook for another five minutes, or until fragrant.
- Stir in the yogurt mixture and bring to the boil. Cook the upma on low heat, stirring continuously, until all the water is absorbed.
- Add the carrot, peas, and lemon juice. Stir gently, adjust the seasoning, and add a little more water if required.
- Cover and cook on a low heat for another eight to ten minutes.
- Transfer to a serving bowl, garnish with chopped coriander and serve hot.

INGREDIENTS

1 small carrot, cut into small cubes

5-6 French beans, chopped

¼ cup shelled green peas, blanched

½ cup sweetcorn kernels, boiled and lightly crushed

½ cup pearl barley

1 tablespoon ghee

¼ teaspoon cumin seeds

1 medium onion, chopped

Mixed Vegetables, Corn and Barley Upma

1 green chilli, slit

½ inch ginger, grated

Salt to taste

2 tablespoons chopped fresh coriander

METHOD

- Soak the barley in two cups of water for half an hour. Drain and set aside.
- Heat the ghee in a pressure cooker.
- Add the cumin seeds. When they begin to change colour, add the onion, chilli and ginger and sauté till the onion becomes soft.

- Add the carrot, French beans, barley and salt. Sauté for two to three minutes.
- Add one and half cups of water. Cover the cooker with the lid and cook till the pressure is released once (one whistle). Open the lid when the pressure has reduced completely.
- Add the green peas and corn kernels and mix. Place on heat and cook for one minute.
- Garnish with the chopped coriander and serve hot.

Hariyali Tikki with Chole

INGREDIENTS

TIKKI

500 grams fresh spinach, blanched and chopped

4 medium potatoes, boiled and mashed

½ teaspoon red chilli powder

½ teaspoon roasted cumin powder

2 tablespoons cornflour

Salt to taste

Oil for shallow-frying

CHOLE

1 cup chickpeas, soaked overnight and boiled till soft

1 large onion, chopped

3-4 green chillies

1 tablespoon coriander powder

1 teaspoon red chilli powder

½ teaspoon turmeric powder

1 teaspoon Garam Masala Powder (page 94)

2 tablespoons oil

1 medium tomato, chopped

Salt to taste

TO SERVE

1 medium onion, chopped

1 medium tomato, chopped

1 tablespoon chopped fresh coriander

METHOD

- For the tikki, mix together the spinach, potatoes, chilli powder, cumin powder, cornflour and salt. Divide into eight portions and shape into tikki.
- Heat the oil in a non-stick frying pan and shallow-fry the tikki till evenly browned on both sides. Drain on absorbent paper.
- For the chole, grind together the onion, green chillies, coriander powder, chilli powder, turmeric powder and garam masala powder.
- Heat the oil in a non-stick kadai. Add the ground paste and sauté for five to eight minutes till well browned.
- Add the tomato and salt, stir well and cook till the oil separates. Add the chickpeas and cook for about five minutes. Add one cup of liquid in which the chickpeas were cooked. Stir well and boil for two minutes. Remove from heat.
- To serve, arrange the tikki on a plate. Top with the chickpeas; sprinkle chopped onion, tomato and chopped coriander. Serve hot.

Cinnamon Raisin Bran Muffins

INGREDIENTS

½ teaspoon cinnamon powder

⅔ cup raisins

1 cup wheat bran

1 cup whole-wheat flour

Oil for greasing

1 teaspoon baking powder

1 teaspoon soda bicarbonate

135 grams butter, melted

¾ cup brown sugar

1 egg, beaten

1½ cups buttermilk

METHOD

- Preheat the oven to 180°C/350°F/Gas Mark 4.
- Grease sixteen muffin moulds with oil.
- Sift the whole-wheat flour with baking powder and soda bicarbonate into a bowl. Add the wheat bran and mix. Mix together the melted butter, brown sugar and raisins.
- Add the beaten egg and mix. Stir in the flour mixture and cinnamon powder. Add buttermilk and mix again. Do not over-mix the batter. It should be lumpy.
- Spoon the batter into the greased muffin moulds till two-thirds full and bake for twenty to twenty-five minutes.
- Cool the muffins in the moulds slightly before turning out onto a wire rack to cool.

Cinnamon Raisin Bran Muffins

Multi-grain Foot-long
with Mushrooms and
Chicken Salami

Multi-grain Foot-long with Mushrooms and Chicken Salami

INGREDIENTS

1 multi-grain long loaf

10-12 medium fresh button mushrooms, sliced

6 chicken salami slices

1 tablespoon oil

Salt to taste

8-10 black peppercorns, crushed

2 tablespoons Mayonnaise (page 95)

8 lettuce leaves, shredded

¼ cup sliced black olives

1 small onion, sliced

5-6 pickled gherkins, sliced

2 cheese slices

Tomato ketchup, as required

Mustard sauce, as required

METHOD

- Heat the oil in a non-stick pan.
- Add the mushrooms and sauté over a high heat for one minute.
- Add salt and the crushed peppercorns. Sauté for one minute longer and remove from heat.
- Slit the bread lengthways without cutting through. Spread the insides with mayonnaise.

- Cover the bottom half with shredded lettuce.
- Arrange the sliced black olives, onion and pickled gherkins on the lettuce. Cut the cheese slices into two and place on the toppings.
- Place the mushrooms and chicken salami on top. Drizzle tomato ketchup and mustard sauce over the filling.
- Press the top half of the loaf down gently to enclose the filling. Cut into smaller pieces and serve immediately.

Oats Cheela with Sprouts Filling

INGREDIENTS

CHEELA BATTER

½ cup rolled oats

1¼ cups gram flour

2 green chillies, chopped

½ teaspoon red chilli powder

¼ teaspoon turmeric powder

½ teaspoon carom seeds

3 tablespoons yogurt

1 tablespoon chopped fresh coriander

Salt to taste

Oil for shallow-frying

Butter, as required

FILLING

1 cup green gram sprouts, blanched and drained

1 tablespoon oil

2 medium onions, chopped

2 medium tomatoes, seeded and chopped

¼ teaspoon turmeric powder

½ teaspoon red chilli powder

½ teaspoon Chaat Masala (page 94)

Salt to taste

1 teaspoon lemon juice

1 tablespoon chopped fresh coriander

METHOD

- To make the cheela batter, mix together the oats, gram flour, chillies, chilli powder, turmeric powder, carom seeds, yogurt, chopped coriander and salt.
- Add one and one-fourth cups of water and whisk to a smooth batter of pouring consistency. Let it rest for ten to fifteen minutes.
- To make the filling, heat the oil in a non-stick pan; add the onions and sauté for two minutes. Add the tomatoes and cook till pulpy.
- Add the sprouts and continue to sauté for half a minute. Add the turmeric powder, chilli powder, chaat masala, salt, lemon juice and chopped coriander and sauté for one minute. Take the pan off the heat and set aside.
- Heat a non-stick tawa; grease it with a little oil and pour a little batter on it. Spread into a thin round with the back of a ladle.
- Drizzle a little oil all around and cook till the underside becomes golden brown. Turn over, drizzle a little oil all around and cook till the other side is equally golden brown.
- Place a portion of the stuffing on one side, fold the other side over to make a half-moon shape. Serve hot with a dollop of butter.

Corn Methi Masala

INGREDIENTS

1½ cups corn kernels, boiled and drained

350 grams fresh fenugreek, chopped and blanched

1 tablespoon oil

1 tablespoon ginger-green chilli paste

4 medium tomatoes, finely chopped

1 teaspoon Kashmiri red chilli powder

1 tablespoon coriander powder

Salt to taste

1 teaspoon dried mango powder

METHOD

- Heat the oil in a non-stick pan; add the ginger-green chilli paste and tomatoes and cook till pulpy.
- Add the chilli powder, coriander powder and salt and mix well.
- Add the blanched fenugreek and drained corn kernels and cook, on medium heat, stirring frequently for three minutes.
- Add half a cup of water, cover and cook for three minutes.
- Sprinkle the dried mango powder and mix well.
- Allow to heat through and serve immediately.

INGREDIENTS

10-12 French beans, cut into ¼-inch pieces

2 medium carrots, cut into ¼-inch cubes

¼ medium cauliflower, separated into florets

¼ cup shelled green peas

2 medium green capsicums, cut into ¼-inch pieces

1 tablespoon coriander seeds

Kadai Vegetables

1 teaspoon cumin seeds

4-5 dried red chillies

12-15 garlic cloves

3-4 green chillies

2 inches ginger

4 tablespoons oil

2 medium onions, sliced

½ teaspoon turmeric powder

1 tablespoon coriander powder

1 teaspoon red chilli powder

3 large tomatoes, roughly chopped

Salt to taste

1 teaspoon Garam Masala Powder (page 94)

3 tablespoons chopped fresh coriander

METHOD

- Grind the coriander, cumin seeds and three red chillies coarsely.

- Grind the garlic, green chillies and half the ginger to a paste. Cut the remaining ginger into thin strips.
- Heat the oil in a non-stick kadai. Add the coarsely ground spice powder and sauté for a while. Add the onions and sauté till golden brown.
- Add the garlic-green chilli-ginger paste and sauté for one minute. Add all the vegetables, except the capsicums, and stir. Cook, covered over low heat, till the carrots are almost done. Sprinkle a little water if necessary.
- Add the turmeric powder, coriander powder and chilli powder and stir-fry continuously. Add the tomatoes, salt and half a cup of water and cook till the vegetables are cooked and the water has dried up.
- Add the capsicums and salt. Cook for four or five minutes over low heat. Sprinkle with garam masala powder.
- Serve hot, garnished with ginger strips and chopped coriander.

Beans Poriyal

INGREDIENTS

250 grams French beans, cut into ¼-inch pieces

2-3 tablespoons oil

½ teaspoon mustard seeds

1 teaspoon skinless split black gram

A pinch of asafoetida

2 dried red chillies, broken into bits

8-10 curry leaves

Salt to taste

¼ cup grated coconut

METHOD

- Heat the oil in a non-stick pan. Add the mustard seeds and split black gram and sauté till the gram turns light brown.
- Add the asafoetida and red chillies and sauté for half a minute.
- Add the French beans, curry leaves and salt. Add half the coconut and mix well.
- Cover and cook over medium heat for five minutes. Garnish with the remaining coconut and serve hot.

Chef's Tip: Use a special coconut grater to get the delicate coconut curls that enhance the appearance of the dish.

Beans Poriyal

Chana and Jackfruit Sukke

Chana and Jackfruit Sukke

INGREDIENTS

1 cup Bengal gram

½ kg unripe jackfruit

1 tablespoon olive oil + for greasing

Salt to taste

½ teaspoon mustard seeds

1 sprig curry leaves

A pinch of asafoetida

1 tablespoon grated jaggery

PASTE

1 teaspoon olive oil

1 teaspoon coriander seeds

½ teaspoon skinless split black gram

¼ teaspoon fenugreek seeds

3-4 whole dried red chillies, broken

1 cup grated coconut

1 tablespoon Tamarind Pulp (page 95)

METHOD

- Soak the Bengal gram in three cups of water for three to four hours. Drain.
- Apply a little olive oil to your palms and knife and remove the skin of jackfruit. Further cut the jackfruit into two centimetres pieces. Apply salt and set aside.
- Steam the jackfruit in a steamer for five minutes. Remove from steamer and set aside.

- Pressure-cook the soaked gram in two cups of water till the pressure is released thrice (three whistles) or till soft.
- For the paste, heat one teaspoon of olive oil in a non-stick kadai. Add coriander seeds, split black gram and fenugreek seeds. Sauté till lightly browned. Add broken red chillies and sauté for a minute. Grind to a coarse paste along with coconut, tamarind pulp and sufficient water.
- Heat one tablespoon olive oil in a non-stick kadai. Add mustard seeds and curry leaves and let the mustard seeds splutter. Add asafoetida and the ground paste. Stir well and cook for two minutes.
- Add boiled gram and stir well. Add the steamed jackfruit, salt and jaggery.
- Stir, add half a cup of water and cook for five minutes on low heat stirring occasionally. Remove from heat and serve hot.

Rajma Masala

INGREDIENTS

1 cup red kidney beans

Salt to taste

2 medium onions, roughly chopped

4-5 garlic cloves, roughly chopped

2 inches ginger, roughly chopped

3 tablespoons oil

¾ teaspoon red chilli powder

1 teaspoon coriander powder

1 teaspoon turmeric powder

5 medium tomatoes, puréed

½ teaspoon Garam Masala Powder (page 94)

½ teaspoon roasted cumin powder

2 tablespoons chopped fresh coriander

METHOD

- Soak the kidney beans overnight in four cups of water. Drain and rinse in fresh water.
- Add five cups of water and salt to the beans and cook in a pressure cooker till the pressure is released four to five times (four to five whistles).
- Grind the onions, garlic and ginger to a smooth paste.
- Heat the oil in a non-stick kadai; add the ground paste and sauté till pale gold.

- Add the chilli powder, coriander powder and turmeric powder, and sauté for two minutes. Stir in the tomato purée and sauté till the oil separates.
- Stir in the kidney beans with two cups of water and adjust salt. Bring the mixture to a boil, lower the heat and simmer, covered, for about ten minutes. Stir in the garam masala powder and roasted cumin powder.
- Garnish with the chopped coriander and serve hot with steamed rice.

Balti Pear Chicken

INGREDIENTS

2 large pears, peeled

800 grams boneless chicken, cut into 8 pieces

1 cup yogurt

Salt to taste

1 teaspoon red chilli powder

1 teaspoon Garam Masala Powder (page 94)

¾ teaspoon turmeric powder

6-7 sprigs of fresh coriander leaves

2 tablespoons oil

4-5 black peppercorns

3-4 green cardamoms

2 bay leaves

1 inch cinnamon

2 dried red chillies

3 medium onions, finely chopped

1 teaspoon garlic paste

2 medium tomatoes, puréed

METHOD

- Pureé one pear and chop the other.
- Marinate the chicken in a mixture of yogurt, salt, half a teaspoon of red chilli powder, half a teaspoon of garam masala powder and the pear purée, for about one hour, preferably in a refrigerator.

- Add one-fourth teaspoon of turmeric powder and mix well. Chop a few sprigs of coriander and add to the marinade.
- Grill the marinated chicken on a barbecue, turning a few times, till evenly cooked. Cut into bite-sized pieces.
- Heat oil in a non-stick balti (kadai) or a non-stick pan; add peppercorns, cardamoms, bay leaves, cinnamon and red chillies. Sauté for a few seconds. Add onions and sauté till golden.
- Add the garlic paste and continue to sauté for a few minutes. Stir in the tomato purée. Add half a teaspoon of turmeric powder and half a teaspoon of chilli powder and sauté for a few minutes more.
- Add the remaining marinade and mix well. Add one cup of water and cook for three to four minutes.
- Stir in the chopped pears. Remove the bay leaf and discard. Roughly tear the remaining coriander leaves and add to the gravy.
- Add the grilled chicken and cook over low heat for three to four minutes.
- Stir in half a teaspoon of garam masala and serve hot.

Lauki Chana Dal

INGREDIENTS

½ small bottle gourd, peeled and cut into 1-inch pieces

½ cup split Bengal gram

Salt to taste

½ teaspoon turmeric powder

1 tablespoon oil

½ teaspoon cumin seeds

2 green chillies, chopped

A pinch of asafoetida

½ teaspoon red chilli powder

2 teaspoons coriander powder

2 medium tomatoes, chopped

½ teaspoon Garam Masala Powder (page 94)

¼ teaspoon jaggery

2 teaspoons lemon juice

2 tablespoons chopped fresh coriander

METHOD

- Soak the split Bengal gram in one and half cups of water for one hour. Drain.
- Cook the split Bengal gram and bottle gourd with salt, turmeric powder and one cup of water till soft.
- Mash lightly with the back of ladle and mix well.
- Heat the oil in a separate non-stick pan.

- Add the cumin seeds, green chillies and asafoetida and cook for one minute. Add the chilli powder and coriander powder and cook till fragrant.
- Add the tomatoes and cook till they soften.
- Add the cooked split Bengal gram and bottle gourd and stir to mix. Add the garam masala powder and jaggery. Lower the heat and cook for two minutes.
- Stir in the lemon juice, garnish with chopped coriander and serve hot.

Lauki Chana Dal

Brown Rice Vegetable Pilaf

Brown Rice Vegetable Pilaf

INGREDIENTS

1½ cups brown rice

2 medium carrots, cut into ½-inch small pieces

10-12 French beans, cut into ½-inch pieces

¼ medium cauliflower, cut into small florets

6-7 medium fresh button mushrooms, halved (optional)

½ cup green peas, shelled and blanched

1 bay leaf

2-3 cloves

1 teaspoon cumin seeds

1 inch cinnamon

Salt to taste

2 green chillies, slit

2 tablespoons fresh coriander, finely chopped

METHOD

- Soak the brown rice in four to five cups of water for two hours. Drain and set aside.
- Heat a deep non-stick pan; add the bay leaf, cloves, cumin seeds and cinnamon and roast for a few seconds or till released.
- Add the drained rice and salt and roast for one to two minutes. Add four cups of water. Bring it to a boil.

- Add the carrots, French beans, cauliflower, mushrooms and green chillies. Stir and bring to a boil. Reduce heat, cover and cook till almost done.
- Add the green peas and mix gently. Cover and cook till done.
- Serve hot garnished with chopped coriander.

Chef's Note: The dish becomes a little sticky on cooking.

INGREDIENTS

½ cup split green gram with skin

1 cup rice

2 tablespoons pure ghee

1 teaspoon cumin seeds

1 inch cinnamon

2-3 green chillies, slit

1 medium carrot, grated

Salt to taste

3-4 black peppercorns, crushed

Chilka Moong Dal Khichdi

METHOD

- Soak the green gram and rice in four cups of water for one hour. Drain.
- Heat the ghee in a pressure cooker; add the cumin seeds, cinnamon, green chillies and carrot and sauté for two minutes.
- Add the green gram and rice and mix well. Add the salt, peppercorns and eight cups of water.
- Cover the cooker with the lid and pressure-cook till pressure is released once (one whistle). Remove the lid when the pressure has reduced.
- Serve hot, with hot melted ghee.

INGREDIENTS

½ cup wheat bran

2 cups refined flour

1 tablespoon fresh yeast

1 tablespoon sugar

1½ cups + 2 tablespoons lukewarm milk

½ teaspoon salt

2 tablespoons oil

1 teaspoon sesame seeds

Bran Bread

METHOD

- Line a baking tray with oiled greaseproof paper.
- Combine the yeast with sugar and two tablespoons of lukewarm water in a bowl and set aside for about fifteen minutes, or until the mixture turns frothy. Stir in the warm milk.
- Place the bran, flour and salt in a mixing bowl. Add the yeast mixture, a little at a time, and mix to form a dough.
- Turn the dough out onto a floured surface and knead for about ten to fifteen minutes, or until the dough is smooth and shiny.
- Cover with a damp cloth and leave in a warm place for about one hour, or until the dough doubles in size.

- Knock back the dough, add the oil and knead again. Divide the dough into two portions, and form each one into the desired shape.
- Place on a baking tray, cover and leave to rise till they double in size.
- Preheat the oven to 220°C/425°F/Gas Mark 7.
- Brush the loaves with a little water and sprinkle sesame seeds over them. Bake for about thirty minutes, or until well-risen.
- The bottom of the bread should sound hollow when tapped. Remove from the oven and transfer to a wire rack to cool. Cut when completely cold.

Bajre ke Bharwan Paranthe

INGREDIENTS

¾ cup millet flour, sifted

¾ cup sifted whole-wheat flour + for dusting

Salt to taste

8 teaspoons roasted sesame seeds

Ghee for shallow-frying

STUFFING

2 medium unripe bananas

Salt to taste

2 green chillies, chopped

1 teaspoon Chaat Masala (page 94)

½ teaspoon red chilli powder

½ teaspoon Garam Masala Powder (page 94)

1 teaspoon chopped fresh coriander

METHOD

- Steam the bananas in their skins in a steamer for seven to eight minutes.
- Peel them while hot and put them in a bowl and mash.
- Add the salt, green chillies, chaat masala, chilli powder, garam masala powder and chopped coriander, and mix well.
- Divide into four equal portions and set aside.

- Mix the millet flour, whole-wheat flour, salt with sufficient water and knead into a soft dough. Divide into four equal portions and roll into balls.
- Sprinkle some whole-wheat flour on the worktop. Place each dough ball and spread gently with fingertips, taking care that the outer edges are thinner than the centre.
- Place a portion of the stuffing in the centre, gather the edges together and seal. Roll into a ball again. Ensure that the stuffing is totally enclosed in the dough.
- Spread the sesame seeds on a plate and press each ball lightly in it on one side only. Roll each of them in whole-wheat flour and place on the floured worktop. Gently spread each ball once again to as thin a parantha as you can.
- Heat a non-stick tawa and lightly grease it. Place each parantha on it, one at a time, and cook for half a minute. Flip it over, drizzle some ghee all around and cook.
- Flip again, drizzle some more ghee all around and cook till both sides are light golden. Serve hot.

Chicken Missi Roti

INGREDIENTS

1½ cups minced chicken

1 cup whole-wheat flour

1 cup gram flour

Salt to taste

1 teaspoon turmeric powder

1 teaspoon chaat masala

4 green chillies, chopped

1 tablespoon dried pomegranate seeds

1 medium onion, finely chopped

2 tablespoons chopped fresh coriander

1 egg

1 tablespoon oil + for shallow-frying

METHOD

- Mix the whole-wheat flour, gram flour, salt, turmeric powder, chaat masala, green chillies, dried pomegranate seeds, onion, fresh coriander, minced chicken and egg. Add a little oil and just enough water to knead into a soft dough.
- Divide the dough into equal portions. Grease your palms and roll the portions into balls.

Chicken Missi Roti

Dal Dhokli

- Heat a non-stick tawa. Roll each ball in some flour and roll out into a thick roti. Place on the hot tawa and cook over a medium heat on both sides.
- Drizzle some oil around the roti and when one side turns golden brown, flip it over and drizzle some more oil, cooking the other side till golden brown. Serve immediately.
- Alternatively, apply a little oil to the dough balls and grease the worktop. With greased fingers, gently pat each ball of dough into a slightly thick roti and cook on the tawa as above.

Bikaneri Dal Parantha

INGREDIENTS

1¼ cups split Bengal gram, soaked

1½ cups refined flour + for dusting

Salt to taste

6 tablespoons pure ghee

¼ teaspoon asafoetida

1 teaspoon coriander powder

1 teaspoon red chilli powder

½ teaspoon Garam Masala Powder (page 94)

Oil for shallow-frying

METHOD

- Combine the refined flour, salt and four tablespoons of ghee.
- Add sufficient water and knead to make a soft, smooth dough. Cover with a damp piece of muslin and rest the dough for ten minutes.
- Pressure-cook the split Bengal gram with two cups of water and salt till the pressure is released two or three times (two or three whistles).
- Remove the lid when the pressure reduces completely and set the gram aside to cool. Grind to a coarse paste.
- Heat the remaining ghee in a non-stick kadai.

- Add the asafoetida, coriander powder, chilli powder and garam masala powder. Sauté for half a minute.
- Add the ground gram and cook for three to four minutes or till dry. Adjust the seasoning and mix well.
- Remove from heat and allow to cool. Divide into eight portions and set aside.
- Divide the dough into eight portions and roll into balls.
- Shape each portion on your palm into a small puri; place a portion of stuffing in the centre, gather up the edges and shape into a ball again. Press each ball down lightly on a work surface. Roll out into a thin parantha, dusting with flour if required. The parantha should be as thin as a papad.
- Heat sufficient oil in a non-stick pan. Slide a parantha gently into the oil and shallow-fry till evenly golden brown on both sides.
- Drain on absorbent paper and serve hot.

Dal Dhokli

INGREDIENTS

¾ cup split pigeon peas

¾ cup whole-wheat flour

2 tablespoons gram flour

Salt to taste

¾ teaspoon turmeric powder

¾ teaspoon red chilli powder

2 pinches asafoetida

½ tablespoon oil

1½ tablespoons raw peanuts

1 tablespoon pure ghee

¼ teaspoon mustard seeds

½ teaspoon cumin seeds

4 garlic cloves, chopped

4-5 curry leaves

3 kokum rinds

1½ teaspoons grated jaggery

2 tablespoons chopped fresh coriander

METHOD

- Soak the split pigeon peas in two cups of water for half an hour.
- Mix the whole-wheat flour and gram flour.
- Add the salt, one-fourth teaspoon turmeric powder, chilli powder, a pinch of asafoetida, oil and sufficient water to knead into a hard dough.

- Roll out thin roti of the dough and cut into diamonds (dhokli).
- Boil the pigeon peas with one and a half cups of water. When half-cooked, add the peanuts and remaining turmeric powder. Set aside.
- Heat the ghee in a non-stick pan; add the mustard seeds, cumin seeds, remaining asafoetida, garlic and curry leaves. Pour the sizzling spices into the dal.
- Add two cups of water and the kokum rinds and bring to a boil.
- Add the jaggery and cook, stirring till the jaggery dissolves. Add the dhokli and cook, stirring occasionally, so that they do not stick to the bottom of the pan. Simmer till the dhokli are cooked.
- Serve hot, garnished with the chopped coriander.

(Image on page 70)

Andhra Dal

INGREDIENTS

1 cup split pigeon peas, soaked

2 unripe bananas, cut into 1-inch cubes

2 teaspoons split Bengal gram, roasted

2 teaspoons coriander seeds, roasted

6-8 black peppercorns

2 teaspoons grated coconut

4 whole dried red chillies

2 tablespoons Tamarind Pulp (page 94)

½ teaspoon turmeric powder

Salt to taste

1 tablespoon chopped fresh coriander

SEASONING

2 teaspoons olive oil

½ teaspoon mustard seeds

½ teaspoon cumin seeds

6-8 curry leaves

A pinch of asafoetida

METHOD

- Pressure-cook the split pigeon peas with unripe bananas and two cups of water till the pressure is released three times (three whistles).
- Grind the split Bengal gram, coriander seeds, black peppercorns, coconut, dried red chillies with tamarind pulp to a smooth paste.

- In a deep non-stick pan, mix together the boiled split pigeon peas, ground paste, turmeric powder and salt.
- Heat the olive oil in a non-stick pan and add mustard seeds. As they begin to splutter add the cumin seeds, curry leaves and asafoetida.
- Pour the seasoning over the pigeon peas mixture and add chopped coriander. Bring to a boil on high heat, stirring constantly. Adjust the consistency.
- Cook for two minutes. Serve hot with rice.

Banjari Dal

INGREDIENTS

⅔ cup split black gram with skin, soaked

⅓ cup split Bengal gram, soaked

¼ teaspoon turmeric powder

Salt to taste

1½ tablespoons pure ghee

2 small onions, sliced

2 cloves

1 inch cinnamon

3 dried red chillies, broken into large bits

1½ teaspoons ginger-garlic paste

1½ teaspoons coriander powder

2 green chillies, chopped

¼ teaspoon black pepper powder

¾ teaspoon red chilli powder

1 tablespoon chopped fresh coriander

1 inch ginger, cut into thin strips

METHOD

- Pressure-cook the split black gram and split Bengal gram together with turmeric powder, salt and three cups of water till the pressure is released four to five times (four to five whistles), or until tender.

- Heat the ghee in a non-stick pan; add the onions, cloves, cinnamon and dried red chillies, and sauté till the onions turn golden.
- Add the ginger-garlic paste, coriander powder, green chillies, pepper powder and chilli powder, and sauté for a couple of minutes.
- Add the sautéed spices to the cooked dal and boil for five minutes. Transfer to a serving bowl.
- Garnish with chopped coriander and ginger strips, and serve hot.

Chilkewali Moong Dal with Palak

INGREDIENTS

¾ cup split green gram with skin

15-20 spinach leaves, roughly shredded

Salt to taste

1 teaspoon turmeric powder

2 tablespoons oil

A pinch of asafoetida

1 teaspoon cumin seeds

2 dried red chillies

2 medium onions, finely chopped

2 green chillies, finely chopped

1 inch ginger, chopped

6-8 garlic cloves, chopped

1 teaspoon lemon juice

METHOD

- Boil the green gram with salt and turmeric powder and three cups of water.
- Heat the oil in a non-stick kadai. Add the asafoetida, cumin seeds and dried red chillies. When the cumin seeds begin to change colour, add the onions and green chillies. Sauté till the onions become soft.
- Add the ginger and garlic and sauté for half a minute. Add the boiled green gram. Bring to a boil and add spinach and lemon juice. Mix well.
- Simmer for two minutes and serve hot.

Char Dal ka Dalcha

INGREDIENTS

¼ cup split Bengal gram

2 tablespoons skinless split red lentils

¼ cup split pigeon peas

2 tablespoons skinless split green gram

1 teaspoon turmeric powder

1½ teaspoons red chilli powder

Salt to taste

1 lemon-sized ball tamarind

3 tablespoons oil

2 medium onions, sliced

2 teaspoons ginger paste

5-6 green chillies, slit

400 grams bottle gourd, cut into 1-inch pieces

SEASONING

2 tablespoons pure ghee

1 teaspoon cumin seeds

5-6 dried red chillies, broken in half

12-15 curry leaves

6-8 garlic cloves, chopped

METHOD

- Soak all the pulses in plenty of water for at least half an hour.
- Drain and place in a pressure cooker with half a teaspoon of turmeric powder, half a teaspoon of chilli powder, salt and four cups of water.

- Pressure-cook for four or five minutes, or till completely cooked.
- Soak the tamarind in one cup of warm water for half an hour. Squeeze out the pulp, strain and set aside.
- Heat the oil in a non-stick pan; add the onions and sauté till light brown. Add the remaining chilli and turmeric powders, the ginger paste and slit green chillies. Sauté for a few seconds and add the bottle gourd.
- Sauté for three or four minutes and add the cooked pulses. Cook, covered over medium heat for about ten minutes, or till the bottle gourd is tender.
- Add the tamarind pulp and half a cup of water and cook over medium heat for four or five minutes, stirring occasionally. Lower heat and simmer for another five minutes.
- For the seasoning, heat the ghee in a small non-stick pan; add the cumin seeds and when they begin to change colour, add the red chillies and curry leaves. Sauté for a few seconds, add the garlic and sauté till the garlic turns light brown.
- Pour the mixture into the dal, cover the pan with a lid immediately to trap the flavours. Serve hot.

INGREDIENTS

½ cup frozen or tinned sweetcorn kernels

¼ cup cream-style sweetcorn

1 cup skimmed milk yogurt

2 tablespoons gram flour

2-3 green chillies, roughly chopped

1 inch ginger

1 teaspoon turmeric powder

2 medium onions, sliced

Salt to taste

Sweetcorn Kadhi

1½ teaspoons oil

¼ teaspoon mustard seeds

½ teaspoon fennel seeds

¼ teaspoon onion seeds

4 dried red chillies, broken into two

METHOD

- Grind together the green chillies and ginger to a fine paste.
- Whisk the yogurt with the gram flour and turmeric powder. Stir in two cups of water and mix.
- Pour the yogurt mixture into a thick-bottomed non-stick pan and bring to a boil.
- Lower the heat and gradually mix in the green chilli-ginger paste, onions and cream-style corn.

- Stir well and cook for two to three minutes. Add the corn kernels, salt and one cup of water.
- Cook over medium heat, stirring frequently, for eight to ten minutes, or till it thickens.
- Heat the oil in a small non-stick pan; add the mustard seeds, fennel seeds, onion seeds and red chillies. Sauté till the spices start to splutter.
- Pour the spices over the kadhi and immediately cover with a lid to trap the flavours.
- Stir well and add the salt to taste. Serve hot with steamed, unpolished rice.

Palak Raita

INGREDIENTS

500 grams spinach

2 cups skimmed milk yogurt

1 green chilli

Black salt to taste

½ teaspoon roasted cumin powder

Salt to taste

METHOD

- Blanch half the spinach in boiling water. Drain, squeeze out the excess water and purée with the green chilli in a blender. Shred the remaining spinach.
- Whisk the yogurt and add the spinach purée, black salt and roasted cumin powder. Mix well and chill in a refrigerator.
- Heat a non-stick pan and add the shredded spinach and cook over high heat for three to four minutes, stirring continuously. Season with salt and mix well.
- Continue to cook over high heat till the spinach is almost dry. Take the pan off the heat and set aside to cool.
- Mix the spinach with the seasoned yogurt just before serving. Add salt to taste and serve chilled.

Pear Chutney

INGREDIENTS

1 large pear

¼ inch ginger, chopped

½ blade mace

½ star anise

½ inch cinnamon

¼ teaspoon salt

¼ teaspoon crushed red chillies

1 teaspoon raisins

1 teaspoon sugar

½ teaspoon vinegar

METHOD

- Chop half the pear and purée the other half.
- Tie up the ginger, mace, star anise and cinnamon in a piece of muslin to make a potli.
- Place the chopped pear in a non-stick pan along with the spice potli, half a cup of water, salt, crushed red chillies, raisins and sugar, and cook on medium heat for about five minutes stirring a few times.
- Add the pear purée and continue to cook for two to three minutes. Add the vinegar and cook till the mixture reduces and gets a chutney consistency. Cool and serve.

Pear Chutney

Lapsi

Cucumber Raita with Flax Seeds

INGREDIENTS

2 medium cucumbers, peeled and grated

1 cup yogurt, whisked

4 tablespoons roasted flax seeds

½ teaspoon roasted cumin powder

Salt to taste

A pinch of Kashmiri red chilli powder

2 tablespoons chopped fresh coriander

METHOD

- Place the cucumbers, yogurt, roasted cumin powder, salt, chilli powder and chopped coriander in a bowl and mix well. Chill in the refrigerator.
- Transfer into individual serving bowls and sprinkle with the flax seeds.
- Serve chilled.

Lapsi

INGREDIENTS

1 cup broken wheat

2 tablespoons pure ghee

3 cups milk

1 cup sugar

1 teaspoon green cardamom powder

6-7 almonds, blanched and slivered

METHOD

- Heat the ghee in a non-stick kadai; add the broken wheat and sauté on low heat till golden brown and fragrant.
- Add the milk and cook on low heat till soft, stirring continuously, so that the milk does not boil over and the mixture does not stick to the bottom of the kadai.
- Add the sugar and cook till the mixture attains a consistency of halwa.
- Add the cardamom powder and mix well. Decorate lapsi with almond slivers and serve hot.

(Image on page 88)

Poached Cinnamon Apples

INGREDIENTS

1 teaspoon cinnamon powder

4 medium apples, cored and kept whole

1 cup unsweetened apple juice

2 tablespoons brown sugar

3-4 tablespoons raisins

2-3 dried figs, chopped

1 teaspoon lemon juice

½ cup red wine

METHOD

- To make the filling, mix together the brown sugar, raisins, dried figs, lemon juice and cinnamon powder.
- Stuff the apples with the filling.
- Prick the apples with a fork. Arrange them on a baking dish and pour over the wine and apple juice.
- Bake in a preheated oven at 170°C/325°F/Gas Mark 3, for thirty to forty minutes.
- Serve warm, chilled or at room temperature.

Gajar aur Khajur ka Halwa

INGREDIENTS

8-10 medium carrots, grated

¾ cup dates, stoned and chopped

1 tablespoon ghee

½ cup sugar

2 cups milk

½ cup crumbled khoya/mawa

4-5 cashew nuts, roughly chopped

½ teaspoon green cardamom powder

10-12 almonds, blanched and slivered

METHOD

- Heat the ghee in a non-stick kadai.
- Add the grated carrots and sugar, and cook for about five minutes.
- Add the milk and continue to cook for six to eight minutes.
- Add the khoya, dates, cashew nuts and cardamom powder, and mix. Cook for ten to fifteen minutes or till almost dry.
- Serve hot decorated with almond slivers.

Chana No Halwo

INGREDIENTS

1 cup fresh green Bengal gram

3 tablespoons ghee

2 cups skimmed milk

2 tablespoons sugar substitute (sucralose)

¼ teaspoon green cardamom powder

¼ cup grated khoya/mawa

10-12 almonds, chopped

10-12 cashew nuts, chopped

METHOD

- Boil the Bengal gram with three cups of water in a non-stick pan or pressure cooker till soft. Drain and grind with a little water to a coarse paste.
- Heat a non-stick pan and add the ghee. When the ghee melts, add the ground gram and sauté till fragrant.
- Add the milk and cook, stirring continuously, till thick. Add the sucralose and cardamom powder, and mix well.
- Add the mawa, almonds and cashew nuts, and cook, stirring continuously, till the mixture thickens and begins to leave the sides of the pan.
- Transfer to a serving bowl and serve hot.

Annexure

CHAAT MASALA

Dry-roast 4 tablespoons coriander seeds, 2 teaspoons cumin seeds and 1 teaspoon carom seeds separately. Cool and powder them with 2-3 whole dried red chillies, 3 tablespoons black salt and ½ teaspoon citric acid. Mix in 1 teaspoon dried mango powder, 1 tablespoon salt and 1 teaspoon white/black pepper powder. Store in an airtight container.

CHICKEN STOCK

Boil 200 grams chicken bones in water for 5 minutes. Drain and discard water. Boil blanched bones with a roughly chopped carrot, celery stalk, leek, 2-3 parsley stalks, 6-7 black peppercorns, 5-6 cloves, 1 bay leaf and 10 cups of water. Remove any scum which rises to the surface and replace it with more cold water. Simmer for at least 1 hour. Remove from heat, strain, cool and store in a refrigerator till further use.

GARAM MASALA POWDER

Dry-roast 10-12 blades mace, 8-10 one-inch cinnamon sticks, 25 cloves, 25 green cardamoms, 10-12 black cardamoms, 2 whole nutmegs, 8-10 bay leaves, 8 teaspoons cumin seeds and 4 teaspoons black peppercorns separately, on a tawa. Cool and grind together all the spices to a fine powder. Store in an airtight jar in a cool, dry place.

GREEN CHUTNEY

Grind together 1 cup fresh coriander, ½ cup fresh mint, 2-3 green chillies, black salt to taste, ¼ teaspoon sugar and 1 tablespoon lemon juice to a smooth paste using a little water if required. Transfer to a bowl and used as required.

MAYONNAISE

Place 1 egg yolk, salt to taste, ¼ teaspoon each white pepper powder, French mustard and sugar and 1 teaspoon vinegar in a clean bowl and mix thoroughly with a whisk. Alternatively, process the mixture in a blender. Add 1 cup of oil, a little at a time, whisking or blending continuously, until all the oil is incorporated. Add 1 teaspoon lemon juice and adjust seasoning. Store in an airtight jar in a refrigerator.

TAMARIND PULP

Soak 75 grams tamarind in 100 ml warm water for 10-15 minutes. Grind to a smooth paste and strain to remove any fibres. Store in an airtight container in the refrigerator.

VEGETABLE STOCK

Peel, wash and chop 1 onion, ½ medium carrot, 2-3 inches celery stalk and 2-3 garlic cloves. Place in a pan with 1 bay leaf, 5-6 peppercorns, 2-3 cloves and 5 cups of water and bring to a boil. Lower heat and simmer for 15 minutes and strain. Cool and store in a refrigerator till further use.

Glossary

English	Hindi
Almonds	Badam
Asafoetida	Hing
Bengal gram, green	Hara chana
Bengal gram, split	Chana dal
Black gram, skinless split	Dhuli urad dal
Black gram, split with skin	Chilkewali urad dal
Black peppercorns	Kali mirch
Bengal gram	Kala chana
Button mushrooms	Khumb/ dhingri
Carom seeds	Ajwain
Chickpeas	Kabuli chane/ chole
Cloves	Laung
Dried fenugreek leaves	Kasoori methi
Dried mango powder	Amchur
Fennel seeds	Saunf
Fenugreek seeds	Methi dana
Mustard seeds	Sarson/rai
Nutmeg	Jaiphal
Olives	Jaitun
Onion seeds	Kalonji
Parsley	Ajmod
Pomegranate kernels	Anar ke dane
Raisins	Kishmish
Sesame seeds	Til
Spring onion	Hare pyaaz
Star anise	Phool chakri/ badiyan
Vinegar	Sirka
Walnuts	Akhrot
Yogurt	Dahi